Pebble® Plus

U.S. SYMBOLS

THE AMERICAN FLAG

by Tyler Monroe

Consulting Editor: Gail Saunders-Smith, PhD

CAPSTONE PRESS
a capstone imprint

Pebble Plus is published by Capstone Press,
1710 Roe Crest Drive, North Mankato, Minnesota 56003
www.capstonepub.com

Library of Congress Cataloging-in-Publication Data
Monroe, Tyler, 1976–
   The American flag / by Tyler Monroe.
      pages cm.—(Pebble plus. U.S. symbols)
   Includes bibliographical references and index.
   ISBN 978-1-4765-3085-7 (library binding)—ISBN 978-1-4765-3507-4 (ebook pdf)—ISBN 978-1-4765-3534-0 (pbk.)
   1. Flags—United States—Juvenile literature. I. Title.
   CR113.M523 2014
   929.9′20973—dc23   2013001820

Editorial Credits
Erika L. Shores, editor; Lori Bye, designer; Svetlana Zhurkin, media researcher; Eric Manske, production specialist

Photo Credits
Alamy: North Wind Picture Archives, 9; Dreamstime: Anthony Aneese Totah Jr., 15; Library of Congress, 13, 17; NASA, 19; Newscom: Image Broker/Carsten Reisinger, 11; Shutterstock: Amy Nichole Harris, cover, Aneese, 21, ArtisticPhoto, 5, Joyce Vincent, 1, Stefan Ataman, 7, Suat Gursozlu (stars), cover and throughout

Note to Parents and Teachers

The U.S. Symbols set supports national social studies standards related to people, places, and culture. This book describes and illustrates the American flag. The images support early readers in understanding the text. The repetition of words and phrases helps early readers learn new words. This book also introduces early readers to subject-specific vocabulary words, which are defined in the Glossary section. Early readers may need assistance to read some words and to use the Table of Contents, Glossary, Read More, Internet Sites, and Index sections of the book.

Printed in China by Nordica.
0413/CA21300509
032013   007226NORDF13

TABLE OF CONTENTS

A National Symbol

Every country in the world
has its own flag. A flag is an
important symbol of a nation.
A flag stands for a country's
land and people.

The American flag is red, white, and blue. It has seven red stripes and six white stripes. It also has 50 white stars on a blue rectangle.

The First Flags

At first the United States was

a group of 13 British colonies.

The Colonies had their own flags.

That changed when the Colonies

joined to fight the Revolutionary War.

An early flag carried by American soldiers during the Revolutionary War was red with a pine tree in the corner.

The Grand Union flag was the earliest flag flown by the 13 Colonies. The flag had a small British flag in the corner and 13 red and white stripes.

In 1777 the Continental Congress passed the first Flag Act. The law created a new flag with 13 stars and 13 stripes.

The United States had grown

to 15 states by 1792. The second

Flag Act passed in 1794.

It said the flag should have

15 stripes and 15 stars.

In 1818 Congress passed the third Flag Act. It said the flag should have 13 stripes. Congress could also add stars as new states joined the United States.

17

The Symbol Today

People fly the American flag in many places. The flag flies outside post offices, government buildings, and schools. There is even a flag on the moon.

American flags are most often

seen on national holidays such as

the Fourth of July and Memorial Day.

The flag reminds people to be

proud of their country.

Glossary

colony—an area that is settled by people from another country and is controlled by that country

Congress—the part of the U.S. government that makes laws; the Continental Congress was the group of leaders that made laws for the American Colonies

government—the group of people who make laws, rules, and decisions for a city, country, or state

Revolutionary War—the American Colonies' fight for freedom from Great Britain from 1775 to 1783; the Colonies later became the United States of America

symbol—an object that stands for something else

Read More

Eldridge, Alison, and Stephen. *The American Flag: An American Symbol.* All about American Symbols. Berkeley Heights, N.J.: Enslow Elementary, 2012.

Harris, Nancy. *The American Flag.* Patriotic Symbols. Chicago: Heinemann Library, 2008.

Mitten, Ellen K. *My Flag.* Little World Social Studies. Vero Beach, Fla.: Rourke Pub., 2011.

Internet Sites

FactHound offers a safe, fun way to find Internet sites related to this book. All of the sites on FactHound have been researched by our staff.

Here's all you do:

Visit *www.facthound.com*

Type in this code: 9781476530857

Super-cool stuff!   Check out projects, games and lots more at
www.capstonekids.com

Critical Thinking Using the Common Core

1. What does the photograph on page 5 show?
   (Integration of Knowledge and Ideas)

2. What role does Congress play in the U.S. government?
   (Key Ideas and Details)

3. Why does the current American flag have 13 stripes?
   (Key Ideas and Details)

Index

Word Count: 244
Grade: 1
Early-Intervention Level: 23